Original title:
The Pocket of Possibilities

Copyright © 2025 Creative Arts Management OÜ
All rights reserved.

Author: Franklin Stone
ISBN HARDBACK: 978-1-80586-060-0
ISBN PAPERBACK: 978-1-80586-532-2

The Veil of Tomorrow's Promise

In my coat there's a treasure, so bold and so bright,
Filled with dreams that dance, like stars in the night.
I pull out a sandwich, its filling a mystery,
Who knew a lunch could lead to such history?

A rubber chicken joins, with a quack and a squeak,
It tells all my secrets, oh what a cheek!
I chase after giggles, they flutter like flies,
Each moment is silly, it's no surprise.

A time machine made of yarn sits inside,
I crochet my regrets, then watch them slide.
My socks hold adventures, with stripes and some dots,
Who knew crazy patterns could tie into knots?

So here in my pockets, absurdity reigns,
With laughter as currency, escape from the chains.
Tomorrow is tempting, with jests on the way,
A whimsically stitched-up, delightful bouquet!

Shimmering Glance into Tomorrow

In my sock, I found a key,
To a world where squirrels skate with glee.
Rainbows dance on jellybean roads,
And ice cream trucks are full of toads.

A trampoline bounces on clouds so high,
Where giggles sprout wings and learn to fly.
Umbrellas that giggle when it starts to rain,
And candy canes delivered by a train.

The Essence of What Lies Ahead

I met a cat who claims to know,
The future of each wiggly toe.
He flicked his tail in a mysterious way,
While offering me donuts made of clay.

A giraffe in glasses reads the news,
About dancing fish in fancy shoes.
He says that time is made of cake,
And each new hour is a slice to take.

The Gentle Tug of Untamed Futures

A robot dog runs my morning errands,
While juggling eggs and stacking lemons.
The grass tickles my feet with its type,
As I sip lemonade flavored with a stripe.

Tomorrow's a bubble that's ready to pop,
With candy floss clouds that fall and hop.
Balloons float by with whispers of cheer,
Telling secrets only penguins can hear.

A Journey Concealed in Threads

I stitched a map with spaghetti strands,
Leading me to beach made of candy lands.
Where gummy bears sail on licorice boats,
And chocolate fish sing high-pitched votes.

A needle pulled through a world of delight,
With thread made from laughter, oh what a sight!
Button blossoms bloom in fields of cheer,
While socks tell tales of the dreams they steer.

Navigating the Unknown

With maps made of jelly and cheese,
I sail through the skies with great ease.
A compass that spins like a top,
The treasures I find, I can't stop.

A cat in a hat sits by my side,
He offers me snacks as we glide.
With each silly tangle and twist,
Adventure and laughter persist.

Possibilities at the Edge

On the edge of a whim, I take flight,
Riding the clouds, feeling just right.
Pigs in sombreros dance with delight,
As rainbows come down, a curious sight.

Jumping on clouds like they're trampolines,
Bouncing on hopes filled with silly dreams.
At the edge of the world, where laughter spills,
I find myself lost in joyous thrills.

Cubes of Curious Fate

In a box of surprises, what do I see?
A monkey with goggles, as bright as can be.
It juggles the planets, oh what a show,
While unicorns dance in the afterglow.

Dice roll like marbles on the floor,
Each tumble reveals something more.
Cubes filled with giggles and dainty little treats,
Every corner, a surprise that repeats.

Spaces for New Beginnings

In a closet of wonders, I open the door,
A parade of socks, just begging for more.
They march with a rhythm, all mismatched and bright,
Creating new styles, oh, what a delight!

Each shoe tells a tale of adventurous roads,
From slip-ups to triumphs, in funny modes.
Spaces where chaos and joy intertwine,
New beginnings are born with laughter divine.

The Embrace of What Could Be

In a sock that lost its mate,
A world of wonders lies in wait.
With rubber ducks in pirate ships,
And popcorn clouds for tasty trips.

A hat that's made of cheese and dreams,
Can grant you luck or silly schemes.
With shoelace ropes we climb so high,
To swing on rainbows in the sky.

Glimmering Fragments of Destiny

A paperclip that bends with glee,
Transforms to magic, oh, you'll see!
While jelly beans conduct the band,
And dance with us upon the sand.

A carrot dressed in formal wear,
Can lead a toast to all that's rare.
With bubbly streams of fizzy fun,
We laugh as night turns into sun.

Threads of Dreams Awaiting to Be Spun

In shoebox forts, we stash our dreams,
With glitter glue and silly schemes.
A rubber band can truly sing,
When wrapped with joy, it makes you spring.

A tangled mess of yarn and cheer,
Can weave a tale that's crystal clear.
With quirky hats and polka dots,
We chase the giggles, tie our knots.

Unseen Paths Beyond the Fabric

A wayward sock slips through the seams,
Where laundry baskets birth our dreams.
With buttons dancing, off they go,
Exploring lands where giggles flow.

A rubber chicken leads the way,
To paths where laughter holds its sway.
With wobbly crayons, we can chart,
A masterpiece from every heart.

Serendipity in Every Fold

In a jacket's nook, dreams take a ride,
A fortune cookie crumb, in stitches, pried.
One sock escapes, it's a tale untold,
In the folds of fabric, adventures unfold.

A hat with a flair, a shoe without mate,
They dance round the room, oh isn't that great?
With humor and chaos, they make quite a scene,
Every crevice's treasure hides something serene.

Threads of Infinite Horizons

A spool of yarn rolls, like troubles in tow,
Knots of mischief in every bright flow.
Stitching a smile, with each clever twist,
Weaving the joy, that no one can miss.

A quirky button leads to far-off lands,
Or a shoelace that ties all the world's hands.
Each thread is a voyage, on life's crazy run,
With laughter in stitches, we bask in the fun.

Celestial Seeds of Potential

In the pocket I find, a star made of cheese,
A galaxy's worth of puns, just to please.
Sprouting confetti, on the sidewalk so bright,
Cotton candy clouds dancing in sheer delight.

A sparkly comet, a fizzy drink pop,
In the depths of our pockets, fun never does stop.
Sowing bright laughter, planting quirks of the day,
With a giggle and wiggle, we're on our way!

Secrets Beneath the Surface

In the lining I find, a napkin of dreams,
With doodles of laughter, and ice cream themes.
A receipt from last week, it's a story so wild,
Of a runaway cat, and a mischievous child.

Buried beneath coins, an old toy soldier,
Whispers of mischief, the pocket's golden holder.
Each secret revealed, gives a chuckle and cheer,
In the depths of our pockets, joy lingers near.

A World Yet to Unravel

In a sock drawer, dreams collide,
A missing sock, the thief inside.
What wonders lay just out of view,
A world unfolds in shades of blue.

Crayons dance and colors blend,
A banana peel becomes a friend.
Towers built from a cereal box,
Giggles echo where logic locks.

Threads of Infinite Tomorrows

A spaghetti strand holds secrets tight,
It whispers tales of pasta fight.
Each twist and curl a story spun,
Of meatballs lost and sauce once run.

The toaster sings with crumbs of fate,
And every slice shall not be late.
With muffins stacked, a tower grows,
What joy in such a floury pose!

Beneath the Soft Fabric of Wishes

A blanket fort, where dreams reside,
Pillow fights and giggles glide.
The cat becomes a knight so bold,
In tales of yarn and treasures told.

Underneath the quilted beams,
We chase away the silliest dreams.
With magic beans and chocolate bars,
The door to joy swings wide, not far.

Dreams Gathered in a Fold

A paper crane takes flight at last,
With hopes and laughter, dreams amassed.
It soars through rooms with open hearts,
Each fold a wish that never departs.

An origami world of glee,
Where penguins wear a tie, you see!
And ice cream trees lined with bright swirls,
Invite all children and playful girls.

Hidden Gates to New Realms

Behind the fence, a door appears,
With squeaks and jigs, it laughs at fears.
A place where socks turn into whales,
And every kite tells wild fairy tales.

A hat that spins when you say 'abracadabra',
Turns your pet cat into a dancing grabber.
Imagine dragons playing chess,
While unicorns wear shirts, oh what a mess!

Secrets Held in Silent Spaces

Beneath the stairs, where dust bunnies play,
Whispers of mischief come out to sway.
A fridge that hums in secret delight,
Hiding ice cream from a midnight bite.

Marbles chatabout their rolling escape,
While shoes engage in a zany capes.
And books that giggle behind the spine,
Wishing for moments just to unwind.

Tucked Away in Time's Embrace

In corners where the old clocks rest,
Time has a snack, it knows the best.
Balloons float freely, trying to dance,
While we sit back and take a chance.

A teacup dreams of flying high,
And whispers about a curious sky.
With each tick and tock, a giggle ensues,
As socks plot journeys in whimsical hues.

Flutters of Chance Between Threads

In tangled yarns, secrets do dwell,
Each stitch a story that tickles as well.
A needle prances, weaving a chat,
While buttons play tag with a curious cat.

Threads of laughter stitch up the air,
While whispers of yarn lead us somewhere.
A sweater's tales warm hearts at night,
In patterns of dreams, oh what a sight!

The Fabric of Now and Then

In the closet lies a coat,
It whispers tales of a goat.
The buttons dance, the threads take flight,
Fashion faux pas sparks delight.

Yesterday's socks wear a grin,
Who knew one pair could hold that spin?
They argue over who's the best,
While the polka dots hilariously jest.

Time's a jester, pulling pranks,
With mismatched shoes and silly flanks.
We stitch together laughs and cheers,
As yarns are woven through the years.

A tapestry of giggles spun,
In threads of chaos, we all run.
Next week's style? A feathered hat!
Oh, the fabric of life is quite the chat!

Glimmers from the Unseen

At dawn, I found a silver spoon,
It giggled softly, 'Let's make a tune!'
We stirred the air with dreams galore,
The unseen world knocked at my door.

Around the bend, a rainbow snorts,
With colors bright in funny sorts.
It says to me, 'Let's paint the skies!'
And laugh along with clouds and skies.

Invisible friends play hide and seek,
They poke my sides and make me squeak.
A glittery wink, a dash of fun,
Through silly antics, we all run.

In the corners of my busy mind,
Glimmers of chuckles, sweet and kind.
The unseen sparkles dance and gleeful,
As laughter stitches joy, delightful!

Conversations with Tomorrow

Tomorrow's hat is filled with dreams,
It whispers secrets in silly themes.
'Let's juggle fruits and ride on mice,'
Each giggle sends a dollop of spice.

Over tea, we chat and grin,
With pastries made from silly sin.
"Will there be unicorns," I say,
And tomorrow winks, "That's child's play!"

Plans are made on pastel napkins,
While laughter bursts with wacky actions.
"Let's bake a cake that sings aloud,"
And hear the tune of tomorrow proud.

Back to today, with crumbs on cheeks,
Life is rich with laughter peaks.
Each moment brims with funny charms,
As tomorrow waves with open arms.

Unfolding the Unexpected

I opened a box of unseen cheer,
And out popped laughter, oh so near.
Surprises danced with pirouettes,
In silly shoes and big blue pets.

Unexpected joy in every fold,
With paper airplanes, stories told.
A rubber chicken on a spree,
Flies past like it's trying to be free.

The clock goes backward, what a sight,
It trips and falls with sheer delight.
As tickles mix with seconds spun,
The hilarity has just begun.

With each unwrapped delight I find,
The giggles weave in perfect kind.
Life's a puzzle; laughter's the key,
In the unexpected, we dance with glee!

The Allure of Uncharted Dreams

In a land where socks roam free,
A parade of mismatched glee.
Pancakes fly, they take a spin,
Chasing rainbows, let the fun begin.

The toaster hums a merry tune,
As waffles dance beneath the moon.
A world where thoughts take silly flight,
With every giggle, hearts grow light.

Unlikely heroes, a pickle and bear,
Plotting adventures, without a care.
Mapping out their tasty quest,
To find the treasure of breakfast best.

So pack your dreams in a toast delight,
And chase those giggles into the night.
Who knew life had so much grace,
When every corner holds a silly space?

Shadowed Footsteps on Untrodden Paths

Sneakers squeak on paths unseen,
While squirrels plot, "What could have been?"
A rubber chicken leads the way,
To realms where jellybeans decay.

Underneath a disco tree,
Dancing ghosts shout, "Come and see!"
They spin in polka dots and cheer,
As pickle hats bring raucous fear.

The road less traveled called my name,
With bubble wrap, it's never lame.
Unseen wonders at every twist,
Like finding cake where no one's missed.

So step right up, the dance begins,
Who knows what joy in chaos wins?
With laughter echoing through the night,
Let shadowed paths give way to light.

Sparks Hidden in Everyday Moments

A spark ignites in morning's glow,
When toast pops up with quite a show.
Jam plays tag on a butter slide,
As breakfast laughter takes a ride.

In the garden, flowers laugh,
Chasing bees, they dance and quaff.
A cat wears shades to steal the scene,
Purring joy like a summer dream.

With socks that dance upon the floor,
Revealing tales of what's in store.
Whiskers wiggle, as if to say,
"Life's a jest; let's play today!"

So grab the moments, they're quite absurd,
Like singing fish or a flying bird.
In every flicker, a giggle found,
In mundane things, joy reigns unbound.

Possibilities Wrapped Tight and Silent

In a cupboard full of mystery,
Lies a rubber duck's history.
Adventures dreamt on quiet shelves,
In secret worlds, we meet ourselves.

Balloons tied tight, waiting to soar,
Whisper dreams behind closed doors.
Lollipop trees with fizzy roots,
Playing hide and seek in colorful boots.

Tightly wrapped, yet bursting free,
Cereal boxes scream with glee.
Who knew silence held such might?
When whispers turned to glitter light.

So unwrap joy and take a bite,
Of life's odd tastes, a sweet delight.
Every secret, a chance to laugh,
In the strange corners of fate's own path.

Crumpled Maps of Hope

In my jacket, treasures lie,
Maps that sway and catch the eye.
Each crease a path, a goofy twist,
Adventure's calling, can't resist!

A treasure marked with coffee stains,
Points to laughter, silly gains.
X marks the spot of missing socks,
Journey starts with funny rocks.

Around the corner, new dreams wait,
Hiccups turn to giggles straight.
With every step, my heart does bop,
Who knows — I just might find a mop!

At the end of this winding track,
Maybe I'll discover my snack.
Maps may crumple, but I still cheer,
While chasing hope, I find good beer!

A Cauldron of Chances

In a pot, I stir my fate,
Mixing laughs, it's never late.
With a pinch of dreams and quirks,
A recipe for silly perks.

Sprinkle in some mischief here,
Giggling potions — never fear!
Stir it up with crazy style,
Every bubble bursts with a smile.

Warts of worry float away,
While chance does a funky sway.
A cackle here, a poppin' sound,
In this cauldron, fun is found!

Soon I'll quaff a brew so bright,
Full of dreams that taste just right.
Laughter boils, the clock's a joke,
Cheers to life, it's all bespoke!

Silhouettes of What Could Be

In the twilight, shadows dance,
Whispering tales of a wild chance.
Figures twirl, absurd and bright,
All the wishes take their flight.

A jester's grin, a pirate's hat,
Silly ideas — imagine that!
Each silhouette a crazy scheme,
Dancing lightly on a dream.

I trace the shapes with ice cream spoons,
Chasing echoes, humming tunes.
What if the moon wore bright red shoes?
Or clouds played hopscotch with the blues?

As shadows fade, the giggles stay,
Sketches of what might come our way.
In this game, we laugh and run,
Tomorrow's glow is just more fun!

Echoes of Unwritten Futures

In the silence, stories hum,
Echoes of futures, full of fun.
A blank page waits, full of glee,
What could happen? Let's wait and see.

Maybe dragons will wear bow ties,
Or robots ponder silly lies.
Every line a giggle stream,
Ink spills forth from wildest dream.

Comets dodging with a grin,
And cats that dance, they always win!
Sipping thoughts from silly mugs,
Crafting tales that wrap in hugs.

So let the stories leap and play,
In this mess of night and day.
For in the echoes of delight,
Are whispered dreams to take flight!

When Possibility Meets Reality

A penguin walks to get a snack,
With a big dream to munch on a Mack.
But he slips on ice in such a mess,
And drags his dreams in a snowy dress.

He dreams of flying high and proud,
But wobbles while the crowd gets loud.
The seagulls laugh, they just can't see,
His heart's a rocket, wild and free.

Turning heads with a waddle's flair,
With hopes that spark in the frosty air.
Reality laughs, a jesting pal,
While he belly flops, a cushy gal.

In a world where wishes like bubblegum stick,
Where laughter's a little oddball trick.
Falling on dreams like goofy clowns,
Who needs a crown when you wear your frowns?

Nestled Visions in a Softfold

In a blanket of thoughts, cozy and tight,
Lies a turtle dreaming of flight.
But the closest he's been to a quicktake-off,
Is bumping his nose on a picnic trough.

A raccoon with plans to start a band,
Strumming his acorns, oh isn't that grand?
But with paws that fumble and glide off key,
He sings for the moon, yet it won't agree.

Marshmallow clouds float in sweet air,
While squirrels critique with a judging stare.
Yet he nods and keeps a grin so wide,
"What's a little off-key?" he said with pride.

Each tucked-away dream is a fluffy couch,
Where funny visions dance and slouch.
Soft smiles bloom in peculiar shapes,
As laughter erupts from wiggly grapes.

Layers of Dreams, Skewed and Unfolded

There's a cat in a hat on a skateboard,
Rolling his way to the fridge, oh lord!
Dreams of a chef with a touch of finesse,
But he just steals fish, leaving a mess.

An owl wearing glasses, books piled high,
Writes poems in flight, oh my!
But on a branch, it's a wobbly scene,
His prose flies off like a fluttering bean.

Bananas tune in, giggling away,
To the silly parables that puppets say.
With every peel, they slip and slide,
In a comedy club where giggles reside.

In layers of laughter, dreams play peek-a-boo,
While absurdities swirl in a vibrant hue.
Unfolding the day with a twist of the odd,
Where silliness reigns, unbound, and unshod.

Inkwell of Unwritten Stories

A quirk in the ink, a pen on the prowl,
Crafting tall tales that giggle and howl.
With stories unwritten, a wild razzle,
Where paper birds dance, a nonsensical frazzle.

A dog in a tutu so brightly mauled,
Steals all the biscuits, yet never feels scrawled.
He twirls and he spins, the showman in town,
Making best friends with the squirrels of brown.

In a world where words leap off the page,
With puns that unravel like a wise sage.
Chaos and giggles, they go hand in hand,
As pages flip-flop and gloriously stand.

So dip in the ink, let the stories unfold,
With whispers of laughter, shades bright and bold.
For every scribble is a fun surprise,
In a universe where absurdity flies.

Distant Melodies of a Wandering Heart

A kazoo plays tunes in the park,
As squirrels dance, leaving a mark.
With jellybeans stuck in my shoe,
I trip on dreams, feeling brand new.

A rubber chicken shakes hands with fate,
While penguins debate what's on their plate.
Confetti falls from the sky so grand,
As fortune cookies swim in the sand.

A dancing cactus sways to the beat,
As socks debate which one's most sweet.
With laughter echoing through the air,
The world's a circus, with jelly to share.

In a hat adorned with a plastic frog,
I find my future in a friendly dog.
With every glance, a surprise awaits,
In the comical dance of chance and fates.

Unraveled Seams and Forgotten Visions

A tattered map points to a pie,
While socks in pairs just wave goodbye.
The threads of fate are tangled tight,
In a game of charades under the moonlight.

Old hats grumble about losing style,
While jelly jars compete in a pile.
A parade of mismatched shoes walks by,
With silly dreams that touch the sky.

A blanket fort hides from the rain,
With gummy bears dancing in the main.
Where socks reveal the secrets they keep,
In a whirl of laughter that makes us leap.

With every pop of a bubblegum burst,
Our wildest thoughts, a comedic thrust.
In the chaos of threads, joy is spun,
As we find delight in the tangled fun.

Moonbeams Tucked In Fabric

A quilt made of dreams that snicker and laugh,
With unicorns knitting, crafting a gaffe.
Stars dance around, trying not to fall,
As jellyfish perform in the hall.

A button wanders, lost from its coat,
While a notebook sings, on a colorful boat.
The fabric soft whispers in silly prose,
With patches of fun where the laughter grows.

The moon's smiling bright, tucked in a patch,
As giggles and secrets the night will hatch.
In this world of whimsy, so grand and wide,
Each stitch a giggle, a joyous ride.

As we roll in the laughter, twirling and twine,
Finding treasure in seams, oh how divine!
With every thread, our fancies inflate,
In the world of fabric, we laugh at fate.

The Cradle of Yet-To-Be-Explored

A treasure chest filled with candy and dreams,
While rubber ducks plot magical schemes.
The clock ticks backward, just for a while,
As bananas dance, wearing a smile.

A pillow fort kingdom, so high and grand,
Where teddy bears hold a rock-band stand.
The crayons gossip, telling tall tales,
Of journeys in shoes with polka dot trails.

A kite takes flight, with a grin so wide,
As cupcakes race on a sugar-filled ride.
In bubbles of laughter, we skip and soar,
In the cradle of wonder, there's always more.

With a wink and a nod, we open the door,
To worlds of adventure where we can explore.
In delightfully silly pursuits we engage,
As life writes the script on a comedic stage.

Plucked from the Universe's Garden

In a garden where dreams grow wide,
I found a fruit, oh, what a ride!
It winked at me with a cheeky grin,
Said, "Pick me now; let the fun begin!"

A veggie comet zoomed past my face,
Nudged by a noodle, abandoned grace.
Lettuce laugh, with tomato on board,
Spaghetti stars twinkled, awards adored!

The sprout of fate beckoned me near,
Whispered secrets I couldn't hear.
With a bite of luck on a potato blend,
I turned to my neighbor, "Let's pretend!"

So here we are, in this garden spree,
With a coffee mug that tastes like glee.
Join the harvest, don't be shy,
Embrace the garden, wave goodbye!

Echoes of Future Adventures

A time machine made of bubble gum,
Took me to places where I'm never glum.
I met a cat in a polka dot tie,
He offered me fish cakes, oh me, oh my!

With jellybean clouds as my cozy seat,
I learned to moonwalk on licorice street.
Dancing with shadows of marshmallow friends,
Laughing so hard, the fun never ends!

Zipping through time on a paper plane,
Avoiding the corner where chores are a pain.
Adventures await, so far and bright,
With each silly giggle, I take flight!

Back to my room, with a pop and a whiz,
I jot down the things that made me fizz.
Each echo resounds, a comedy play,
In the theater of dreams, let's laugh all day!

Crumpled Aspirations and Inked Lines

I scribble dreams on crinkled page,
With a hopeful heart in a scribbly rage.
Each aspiration like a wayward kite,
Flying in circles, oh, what a sight!

My pencil danced with charcoal flair,
Wrote a novel involving a bear!
He wore a hat made of crayon hues,
Searching for socks, mine, not his shoes!

The coffee spilled; rewrote fate's script,
An inkblob adventure, reality flipped.
With each crumple, I laugh and learn,
In the chaos, my chances churn!

So here's to the lines, both straight and bent,
For every mishap, a giggle's scent.
Life's a story, twisted and fun,
Dance through the errors, life's well begun!

Stitched Together by Serendipity

A patchwork quilt of serendipity,
Made from scraps of pure spontaneity.
With mismatched colors that laugh and cheer,
Each stitch a memory, gathering near!

Tangled threads of fortune's delight,
Knitted on evenings when laughter was bright.
I found a sock in a spaghetti strand,
Whispered, "Let's travel!" and off we planned!

With buttons of joy and a zipper of hope,
We sewed a cape to help us cope.
As breezes painted stories untold,
In this patchwork life, we are boldly sold!

Together we weave, laugh, and create,
With each quirky twist, we celebrate fate.
So here's to the fabric of shared delight,
A dance of serendipity, shining bright!

Pockets of Laughter in a Stitched World

In a world of stitches, I find a seam,
A pocket of jokes, bursting at the beam.
Socks argue with shoes, who's the funnier pair?
Even zippers are giggling, unaware of the snare.

Buttons have meetings, oh what a sight!
Discussing the humor in fabric at night.
A patch that can laugh, now that's quite the find,
Tailors chuckle softly, their humor well-lined.

Moments Curled Up with Possibility

Curled up on the couch, dreams start to hum,
Ideas bounce like puppies, wagging with fun.
A blanket of whimsy, cozy and bright,
Swapping dull thoughts for a tickle or slight.

Oh, popcorn in pockets, what a bizarre snack!
Each kernel a chance on a serendipity track.
Sipping on laughter, it's served up hot,
In moments of joy, we connect the dot.

Enigmas Held Closely

In the closet of secrets, my socks play the game,
Hiding their partners, it's never the same.
What happened to strays? They giggle and tease,
Each mismatched pair holds a riddle with ease.

The coats whisper tales when no one is near,
Of romps in the rain, still they dry without fear.
Scarves have their stories, of twirls in the breeze,
All holding enigmas, like candy in trees.

The Fabric of What Is Yet to Manifest

A tapestry woven, with threads full of cheer,
Each stitch tells a tale of the dreams drawing near.
With feathers and glitter, a splash of delight,
Manifesting giggles that dance in the night.

The fabric is vibrant, with colors that chime,
A rhythm that tickles, syncopates time.
Who knew that creation could wear such a grin?
In this silly parade, the fun is a win!

Whispers of Hidden Dreams

Socks that never found their pair,
Under beds they float in air.
Goldfish wish they had a boat,
In a bowl they learn to float.

Old maps with routes that twist and turn,
Show us places we can yearn.
A half-eaten cake calls us to play,
Hiding secrets of yesterday.

Jumping puddles in rain galore,
Let's build castles on the floor!
A spoon's a spaceship, don't you see?
Adventure lies in cups of tea.

Clocks that tick in jumbled rhyme,
Chasing giggles, losing time.
Each tick a chance for mischief new,
In laughter, dreams come true!

Fragments of Untold Journeys

A sandwich finds a way to dance,
In lunchboxes it takes a chance.
With pickles as its loyal crew,
They set sail, just for the view.

Left shoes waltz with right in pairs,
Chasing thoughts through tangled hairs.
A lion roars in a child's smile,
On walls adorned with crayon style.

Backpacks stuffed with fuzzy toys,
Setting off to find the noise.
Maps made of ice cream melt away,
On sunny days that dare to sway.

Cups of giggles spill on the floor,
As dreams run wild and beg for more.
With no destination in mind,
We're off to see what we can find!

Shadows of Unlived Moments

Balloons that float to say hello,
To silly thoughts just passing slow.
Clouds shaped like turtles drift right by,
Whispering jokes to the sky.

A broomstick rides on winds of flair,
Chasing dust bunnies in the air.
Potatoes play hide and seek,
In the pantry, not so bleak.

Invisible capes we're wearing bright,
Twirling around in sheer delight.
With every step, a quirky dance,
Life's too short to miss the chance.

Jellybeans offer daring thrills,
In candy land, with endless chills.
Let's skip through shadows of our dreams,
With laughter bursting at the seams!

Tucked Away in Tomorrow

A butterfly dreams of being a plane,
With wings that sing in the rain.
Giggles tumble down the street,
With every bounce, a new heartbeat.

Jellyfish wear hats and twirl,
Inviting seaweed for a whirl.
In this realm of snails and eyes,
Adventure's just a sneeze away, surprise!

A cat debates a sunlit spot,
Should it nap or twist a knot?
Each day's a mix of fun and tease,
Where time can bend with such great ease.

Tomorrow's tucked in yesterday's sleeve,
Whispers of wonders that we believe.
Let's chase the sun till it's all gone,
With laughter ringing on and on!

Lurking Meanwhile in Stitches

A cat in a hat, oh what a sight,
Chasing its tail from morning to night.
With each little tumble, the giggles arise,
As yarn balls roll out, oh what a surprise!

A mouse in a sweater, wearing a grin,
Sneaks past the dog, what a curious win.
He dances on counters, stealing a bite,
While the dog just snoozes, dreams soft and light.

The clock's ticking fast, but who cares to wait?
When you're crafting mischief, it's never too late.
With needles and laughter, we stitch up the day,
In this world of whimsy, come join in the play!

In this fabric of fun, no seam is too tight,
We'll unravel the worries, let's dance in delight.
So grab all your friends, let's spin tales galore,
Lurking meanwhile brings laughter and more!

The Thread of Fate Yet to Weave

A squirrel with glasses, a scholar profound,
Calculates acorns he gathers around.
He's mapping each branch with such careful thought,
Until a big bird says, "What have you brought?"

The jeans with patches, a fashion quite bold,
Bouncing on bicycles, laughter untold.
Each rip tells a story, a tumble or two,
While patchwork friends giggle, and join in the zoo.

With every short snicker, a fortune might bloom,
For fate's a loose thread in a cluttered room.
Twisting and turning, the fabric will change,
We'll stitch up our dreams, they're never too strange!

So let's twirl the thread, oh what will it be?
A map to adventure, or a riddle of tea?
With a needle of jokes, we'll make our own fate,
And dance through the stories, oh isn't it great?

Shards of Light in Enveloping Darkness

In shadowy corners where giggles reside,
A glowstick brigade is ready to slide.
They dance in the darkness, glowing so bright,
While munching on popcorn, it's pure sheer delight.

An owl with a quirk, a wise little chap,
Whispers amusing tales, and naps in his cap.
"Remember, dear ones, to always bring cheer,
For laughter's the lantern that chases out fear!"

A jigsaw of surprises, pieces in hand,
We'll build up our hopes, and make merry plans.
With puzzles and laughter, the night feels so grand,
While shards of bright giggles together will stand.

So light up your lanterns, let joy navigate,
In corners of fun, we all celebrate.
With each silly riddle, we'll banish the gloom,
Shiny sparks of laughter will burst in the room!

Soft Echoes of Unlived Lives

In the attic, a hat stands tall on a shelf,
Whispers of wonder, it longs for some help.
A time-traveling dreamer, it yearns for some air,
With tales of adventures, oh, what a flair!

A pair of lost socks, with stories untold,
Once danced on the floor, now waiting, so bold.
Wrapped in sweet memories, they giggle and sigh,
Imagining journeys they'd take if they'd try.

An umbrella with charm, it dreams of a storm,
Ready for puddles where laughter takes form.
It rustles and giggles, and spins in delight,
As raindrops come tumbling to shimmer through night.

So reflect on the silly, the lives left unseen,
Each echo a treasure, and laughter between.
With soft hints of joy in lives we can't find,
We cherish those whispers and let love unwind!

A Dance with the Unexplored

In a world where chickens fly,
I wear a hat made of pie.
The moon wears socks on its feet,
As squirrels all dance to the beat.

A cat plays chess in the tree,
While a dog sings in harmony.
Jumping over clouds made of cream,
We laugh at this silly dream.

An octopus plays with a kite,
While a turtle joins in the fight.
They argue over who can run,
But no one wins; it's all just fun.

In this dance, we twirl and spin,
With every giggle, we all win.
So let's take a chance, my friend,
In this waltz that will never end.

Hues of Tomorrow in a Sleeved Pocket

I found a rainbow in my sleeve,
It giggled at the tricks we weave.
A pickle hat perched on my head,
Whispers secrets it never said.

Chasing lemons that wear shoes,
While jellybeans sing the blues.
In color, we dip and dive,
In this world, we feel alive.

A cupcake rides on a hot-air balloon,
Waving hello to the silver moon.
We paint the sky with spaghetti dreams,
While everything bursts at the seams.

With every hue, we laugh and play,
Twisting time in a jolly way.
In pockets deep, we store our cheer,
Only to share it throughout the year.

Whirls of Fortune Just Beyond Reach

There's a fortune cookie in my hat,
It told me I'd outsmart a cat.
With a wink, I jumped through a hoop,
Where donuts dance in a jolly group.

Mistakes are just cake that we eat,
While juggling shoes on our feet.
Hiccups turn to laughter, you see,
As we tumble over that bouncy tree.

Frogs in tuxedos play the fiddle,
And prance about without a riddle.
We spin through time on a yo-yo thread,
Where goofy socks on our feet are wed.

So here we spin, just out of reach,
On slides made of candied peach.
With giggles, we conquer what we lack,
Hand in hand, never looking back.

Spaces Between the Threads of Life

In spaces where giggles reside,
The socks and shoes have a pride.
Whiskers tickle the morning dew,
As cats put on a dance review.

The spaghetti grows really tall,
While marbles bounce against the wall.
Life's a game, a silly chase,
In this whimsical, wacky place.

Jumping on clouds made of fluff,
Where laughter is more than enough.
Caught in the weave, we twirl and swoop,
With every twist, we form a group.

So let's embrace this crazy thread,
With smiles that won't stay in our head.
In the spaces between each laugh,
We find the joy that's our other half.

Unfolding Potential in Every Stitch

A button here, a patch over there,
My pants are now a masterpiece rare!
With every thread, a tale untold,
Fashion fails, but laughter's gold.

Zippers that stick, and seams that fray,
Creating styles in a wobbly way!
My closet's a circus of colors and whim,
Don't ask why my jacket is missing a hem.

Socks that don't match are the new chic
Cloth that squeaks—oh, what's that peak?
I'll strut my stuff with quirky flair,
Wardrobe mishaps, but who even cares?

Through fabric and fun, my skills adrift,
Each timeless outfit a comical gift.
For in this chaos, we find the truth,
Style over sense? Well, that's just proof!

The Map of Unseen Journeys

With crayons drawn, paths diverge,
The coffee's cold, yet dreams emerge.
A scribbled line from here to there,
With every twist, a mishap to bear.

The signposts say 'teacup rides',
But I'm lost in the world of odd slides!
Maps in pockets, treasures unknown,
Navigating chaos like a bumbling drone.

X marks the spot of my next grand quest,
Finding the ice cream truck—it's for the best!
But who needs maps when you've got glee,
Just follow the laughter, that's the key!

Lost at sea or found on land,
Uncovered joys are always so grand.
Each misstep a giggle, every turn a delight,
With a map made of dreams, we'll be alright!

Nestled Among the Ordinary

In a world of socks and half-eaten fries,
I find my joy hidden in pies.
The mundane sparkles, oh what a thrill,
A cat on a chair? Let's climb that hill!

Magic in laundry and crumbs on the floor,
Potatoes make the best dance floor!
With each silly moment, a treasure unfolds,
In the heart of the chaos, laughter beholds.

The neighbor's dog wears a silly hat,
It's just a Tuesday; imagine that!
As flowers bloom in the laundry bin,
Life's little quirks make me grin.

Sometimes a mess is a story's seed,
In the ordinary, there's fun indeed.
So embrace the chaos, and don't be shy—
For nestled within, the joys always lie.

Dreams Cradled in Cotton

In soft cotton sheets, my dreams take flight,
Pillow fights turn into glorious night!
I toss and I tumble, the blanket's alive,
A cotton candy world, where giggles thrive.

Nightmares tiptoe in on sneaky feet,
But I fight back with my dance retreat!
Cuddled in fluff, the moon starts to smile,
Every dream's vibrant, enclosed in style.

If dreams were socks, I'd wear them both,
With polka dots that prevent me from growth!
In the dreamland of whims, let's simply roam,
Each fantasy woven, a fabric from home.

So here's to the nights that sparkle and gleam,
Where silliness flows and evokes a dream.
In cotton we trust, for laughter and rest,
With whimsy at heart, I am truly blessed!

Curated Moments of Magic

In a world where socks can dance,
And teapots sing a lively prance,
I found a spoon with wings, oh dear,
It said, 'Chase your whims, have no fear.'

A cat wearing a monocle sits,
Debating the pros of cheese and bits,
He flips a coin, it lands on 'me',
Now he's the boss, my life's a spree.

Balloons with faces, giggle and sway,
As pancake stacks shout, 'Eat us today!'
The fridge opens wide, it's a dance hall,
Where yogurt and pickles throw a ball!

I caught a laugh, it wriggled and slipped,
Tamed it with joy, and then it flipped,
Now I keep it in my warmest sock,
Quick, let's find the next silly clock!

The Corner of Dreams and Reality

In a realm where narwhals juggle pies,
And toast on trampolines aims for the skies,
I met a frog in a three-piece suit,
Who offered me candy in exchange for a flute.

An octopus played the ukulele,
Dancing in rhythm—not too swaley,
While a clam in shades sold shells of luck,
Shouting, 'Buy one today, or you're out of pluck!'

The clouds wore hats made of cotton candy,
Tickling the sun; heavens were dandy,
While rain started humming a tune so sweet,
My umbrella danced to the beat of its feet.

In this place where silliness reigns,
A bicycle rides on tracks made of trains,
I snatched at dreams, caught a few bright,
And held them tight till they burst into light!

Embers of Hope Wrapped Tight

A squirrel in pajamas sips from a cup,
Saying, 'Hey, why not just shake it up?'
With a nod to the moon, all stars convene,
And play hopscotch on a twinkling sheen.

Rusty old bikes sprout wings and fly,
Chasing down cupcakes tossed from the sky,
With every bite, a giggle ensues,
As rainbow sprinkles dance in their shoes.

A hedgehog reads riddles to passing clouds,
While jellybeans rock in vibrant crowds,
The sun just rolled its eyes in delight,
'Grow a little sillier, goodnight—goodnight!'

In this haven where laughter ignites,
I wrapped my hopes in cozy delights,
So when I unwrap them, let joy ignite,
And turn every moment into pure light.

Tiny Vessels of Wonder

I found a jar where giggles reside,
With a pop and a fizz like a cozy bide,
It sparkled and shimmered, full of delight,
Each flicker a dream that danced in the night.

A snail with a cape zoomed past on a ride,
Proclaiming himself the best on the slide,
While paper planes soared over tall trees,
Filling the air with their whimsical pleas.

The mushrooms play chess with the bees all around,
As four-leaf clovers leap up from the ground,
A party erupts with sweets and with song,
Where everyone laughs, and nothing feels wrong.

So gather your wonders, big and small,
For joy has a way of making you feel tall,
These tiny vessels, they bounce and they spin,
Wrap them in laughter, let the fun begin!

Shades of Dreams Caught in Stitches

In a quilted world of misfit seams,
A cat walks by, plotting its schemes.
With buttons for eyes and thread for a grin,
Who knew such magic could come from a tin?

A squirrel in socks flaunts its flair,
While pigeons in bowties strut with care.
Each stitch a giggle, each patch a cheer,
In this wild fabric, there's nothing to fear.

The toaster sings as it burns the bread,
While dancing spoons dream of being fed.
In a pocket of laughter, we all collide,
Stitching up fun, with joy as our guide.

So toss your worries in a playful sling,
Let whimsy happen, oh what a fling!
The world is a canvas, so paint it bright,
With shades of dreams in the morning light.

The Carried Weight of Ambition

With a briefcase stuffed with hopes and dreams,
A penguin waddles, or so it seems.
His tie is crooked, his hat askew,
Ambition is heavy, but gives him a view.

A jellybean's job is to spread cheer,
While a snail claims its corner, "I'm the premier!"
With to-do lists written on fish scale sheets,
They march on forward, amidst the defeats.

In the hustle and bustle, they trip and they fall,
Each tumble a lesson, a giggle, a call.
Heavy on dreams, but light as a whisper,
They carry their goals, like a fluffy old lizard.

Like juggling puppies in a circus show,
They dance with their dreams, putting on a glow.
Ambition's a weight but isn't a chore,
As laughter spills out, they always want more.

In the Curl of a Silken Dream

A shoelace unfurls with a swish and a twirl,
While cinnamon rolls dance and twirl.
A whisper of silk floats through the air,
"Catch me if you can, if you dare!"

A feathered hat tips in a playful way,
To the beat of the dreams that want to play.
Marshmallow clouds giggle as they drift,
In the curl of a dream, life's full of gift.

With a wink of a star, the night sings a tune,
Frogs in tuxedos are out to commune.
In slippers of comfort, they shuffle and sway,
Wrapped in the magic where dreams come to play.

Life's a delightful, serendipitous game,
Full of silk ribbons and laughter untamed.
So spin in the joy, let your heart take flight,
In the curl of a dream, everything feels right.

Footprints Beneath the Skirt of Time

With flip-flops clapping on a sunny street,
They dance on echoes, with jigs and feet.
A turtle with shades thinks it's all a race,
Trailing behind, moving with grace.

The moon whispers secrets to the goofy pine,
While ants in a line plot their next design.
In the silliness of hours, quirks intertwine,
Footprints scatter, where laughter aligns.

A clock leans back and gives a loud yawn,
As jellybeans sing their goofy little dawn.
With each tiny step on the path of the grind,
We carve out our stories, forever entwined.

So here's to the capers, the slips, and the falls,
The footprints that echo in party halls.
Beneath the skirt of time, we make our own rhyme,
With laughter as currency, we dance on a dime.

Lanterns in the Mist of Uncertainty

In a fog where socks go roam,
A playful ghost claims our home.
With lanterns bright, we shine the light,
On silly quirks that dance in night.

Who knew my shoe could disappear?
Maybe it's off to grab a beer!
While I chase shadows, oh what fun,
Laughing loud at what we've spun.

The cat's a spy, atop the shelf,
Plotting schemes all by herself.
With tiny paws on secret trails,
She whispers plans of silly tales.

So here we stand, a merry crew,
With laughter shared and dreams anew.
In misty moments, we just might,
Find treasures hidden from our sight.

Chasing the Breeze of Change

On a kite made of laughter, we sail,
Riding winds that tell a tale.
With giggles swirling all around,
Every twist brings joy profound.

The neighbor's cat, a jokester sly,
Watches with an amused eye.
As change unfurls its playful dance,
We leap and twirl, embrace the chance.

The trees all bend to hear our cheer,
As whispers of adventure near.
Let's trade our fears for silly hats,
And dance with clouds while playing spats.

In every breeze, a new surprise,
We discover joy in the skies.
With every gust, let's sprint and shout,
For change is what life's really about.

Windows to Whimsical Ventures

Through windows wide, our dreams take flight,
With wiggly worms that sparkle bright.
We launch our hopes like rubber bands,
Soaring high above the lands.

A squirrel steals our lunch with glee,
Dressed in shades, as cool as he.
We chase him down with jelly jars,
Through gardens sprouting candy bars.

In this land of odd delight,
We cartwheel into the moonlight.
With giggles shared on every block,
We scribble tales on walls of chalk.

Let's peek through every funny pane,
Uncover secrets, wild and insane.
In whimsical ventures, we will find,
A world that's playful and unconfined.

Surprises in the Seat of Silence

In the corner where the dust bunnies breed,
Reside surprises that all plants need.
A whoopee cushion sings its tune,
As quiet moments leave us strewn.

The goldfish pondering life's great schemes,
Dreams up adventures in vibrant beams.
While I sip tea with a biscuit friend,
A chuckle escapes as worries bend.

Underneath still waters' face,
Fish with mustaches play a race.
We watch in awe, our hearts a-flutter,
As giggles burst like caps of butter.

In silence, magic starts to bloom,
Whispers of joy disperse the gloom.
So next time stillness makes you yawn,
Remember laughter's never gone.

Echoes of Tomorrow's Laughter

In a jacket too tight, I found some old fries,
A treasure from lunch that had traveled the skies.
Broke out into giggles, as they danced with the grime,
Who knew that stale snacks could be fun every time?

Balloons in my pocket, though they've long lost their air,
Still bounce off my thoughts, floating here and there.
They whisper of giggles, of silly balloon fights,
Like echoing laughter that sparks up the nights.

An old rubber chicken, now faded and bent,
Quacks jokes that my childhood had more than content.
I tell it my secrets, it cackles away,
Time flies when you're laughing, or so they say!

With socks full of dreams and a hat full of jest,
I stumble through moments, in silliness dressed.
For tomorrow invites us, with big, goofy eyes,
To clutch at the laughter, and wear it like ties.

Whispers of Unwritten Dreams

In the folds of my jacket, ideas take flight,
Paper cranes, origami, in colors so bright.
With scribbles of nonsense, they fluttered and swayed,
Ignoring my logic, they boldly delayed.

A crumpled-up napkin with plans for a band,
We'll play all the songs that no one ever planned.
With spoons for guitars and a drum made of cheese,
Our concerts are wild, with laughter to please.

An eraser that wore a mustache one day,
Swore it knew magic in a whimsical way.
It bounced on the table, the jester of dreams,
Bringing giggles and chortles, or so it seems.

With vacant notebooks, where ideas will sprout,
Each line is a whisper, an amusing shout.
For in the realm of dreams, silly thoughts reign,
Unwritten, they hover, like clouds in the rain.

Endless Horizons in My Hand

A compass that spins, with no sense of direction,
Confetti directions, a laughable collection.
Took a wrong turn, but who's keeping the score?
Adventures are better when you're lost at the core.

Bubbles of plans floating high in the air,
They pop with a giggle, with laughter to spare.
Each burst brings a smile, a joyfully wild twist,
In the realm of nonsense, we find what we missed.

Marbles of fortune, in pockets they jingle,
Each one a story, a riddle to mingle.
They might just roll out, on a quest of their own,
Leading to folly, where silliness's grown.

Each new curiosity, a riddle to tease,
The world is a playground, filled with giggles and ease.
With horizons of fun held tight in my hand,
Endless are the joys when we're living unplanned!

Secrets Beneath the Surface

In my shoe, there's a secret, it flaps like a fish,
Whispering tales of a mystical wish.
It swims through my thoughts, while I'm stuck in a line,
Collecting the giggles, like bubbles of brine.

Under the surface, where oddities dwell,
A shoelace that raps, has a story to tell.
With knots and with twists, it binds dreams so tight,
Creating a dance in the soft, moonlit night.

A pebble I pocketed, smooth as can be,
Claims to be wisdom, all wrapped up for me.
It whispers in riddles, though I can't comprehend,
The humor of stones that pretend to be friends.

Mysteries linger, like candy in jars,
With laughter as fuel, we can reach for the stars.
For secrets, they're silly, they're winks in disguise,
When laughter uncovers the truth in our eyes.

Veils of Hidden Aspirations

Beneath my bed, a sock I find,
Where dreams of grandeur often bind.
A crumpled note, a rubber band,
Unraveled hopes at my command.

My closet hides a pirate's map,
Or maybe it's just an old mishap.
With dusty boxes stacked so high,
Who knows what treasures could reply?

A lawn chair's seat holds my career,
As I nap beneath the sky, my dear.
Each snore a venture, bold and loud,
While cats convene, my secret crowd.

Those whispers late at night conspire,
To pull me from my cozy mire.
"Come chase the moon, it's not too late!"
So off I go to change my fate!

Archways to New Dimensions

The door creaks wide, a robot peers,
Is this reality or just cheers?
I step right in and lose my shoes,
Dancing with aliens, what a ruse!

A toaster flies, it warms my toast,
With every bite, I start to boast.
"Just flick the switch," I boldly state,
And find a portal, isn't that great?

Two-dimensional cats, they meow,
They want to join the fun right now.
With every leap, I gain a friend,
Imagination knows no end!

We sail through stars, a banana boat,
With giggly fish that love to float.
Such silly worlds we're bound to find,
Adventure flows, laugh-unwound!

The Soft Whisper of Unseen Light

In shadows deep, a giggle glows,
A tangle of dreams, a tangled prose.
They whisper secrets, soft and neat,
While I trip over my dancing feet.

A sprinkle of joy, a sprinkle of glee,
A glow-in-the-dark fruit from a tree.
With lemon zest and a wink of fate,
I leap into a crystal plate.

The kitchen sings with pots and pans,
They tap-dance like the best of bands.
I join the rave, with spoons and forks,
All creatures cheer as laughter sparks.

Each twilight glance reveals what's best,
The whimsy hidden in a jest.
So embrace the light that plays the fool,
For magic winks in every pool!

A Treasure Chest of What Cannot Be Named

A chest beneath my bed of dreams,
Holds mysteries more than it seems.
With shiny buttons, bits of string,
It harbors tales of random bling.

A rubber duck, his quack so sly,
Claims he's a spy from the nearby sky.
A cookie crumbles, oh what a heist,
And giggles echo like a feast, not sliced!

Old crayons whisper bright ideas,
Like rocket ships and new careers.
With every stroke, a world takes flight,
The laughter shines, an endless sight.

As I dig deeper, I find a tune,
A kazoo's serenade beneath the moon.
What cannot be named may speak so loud,
In silly treasures, I'm ever proud!

Petals of Ambition in the Wind

In a garden of dreams, we frolic and dance,
Chasing after whims, oh what a chance!
With petals for wings, we float on a breeze,
Laughing at limits, as we do as we please.

A jester's cap perched, ideas all around,
Nonsensical plans in giggles abound.
Sprouting like daisies, our thoughts take a leap,
Into grand schemes that keep us from sleep.

Who knew a wild thought could sprout like a vine?
Twisting and turning, oh isn't it fine?
From puddles of giggles, new visions emerge,
Tickling our fancies, like popcorn we surge.

With laughter as fuel, we zoom to new heights,
Racing our shadows, engaging in flights.
In this garden of whimsy, we flourish, so free,
Petals in hand, we're as bold as could be.

Uncharted Paths of Innovation

Maps made of squiggles, we chart out our quest,
With markers of laughter, we plan for the best.
Innovation's a game, no need for a guide,
Let's roll up our sleeves, and go take a ride!

Invention's a circus, with clowns in their prime,
A sprinkle of chaos, a dash of sublime.
We juggle our hopes, as ideas take flight,
Building castles in air, what a wonderful sight!

Exploring the wacky, the weird and the wild,
Who knew that the truth could be so beguiled?
With giggles as our compass, here we boldly roam,
Finding sweet treasures, we call it our home.

Turning left into laughter, right into cheer,
With friends all around, there's nothing to fear.
The journey's our canvas, let colors collide,
Unearthing new wonders, with joy as our guide!

Shadows of Serendipity

In the moonlight's glow, shadows frolic and play,
Unexpected moments dance in disarray.
Tripping on laughter, we giggle anew,
Stumbling on joy, oh how it just grew!

A slip on a banana, a cartwheel gone wrong,
Serendipity shines in our sing-along song.
With each little fumble, we find surprise,
Unraveled adventures, beneath twinkling skies.

The past gives a wink, as the present takes heart,
Mapping our mischief, with laughs as our art.
How lucky indeed, with each twist of fate,
To find joyous wonders, that just can't wait!

So let's dance with mistakes, embrace every blunder,
In shadows of whimsy, we'll create a wonder.
Serendipidous magic, we'll paint all around,
In the corners of life, joyfully found!

Beyond the Boundaries of Dreams

With dreams like balloons, we rise up with glee,
Soaring over rooftops, as light as can be.
The sky's not the limit, but merely a clue,
For all that we imagine, can become something true.

Waking up giggling, we sketch our delight,
Turning whims into whimsies, our visions take flight.
With crayons of laughter, coloring wide,
Beyond the odd edges, we take every stride.

Building bridges with wishes, we skip through the air,
Sailing on moments, no reason to care.
Beyond boundaries drawn, our souls are so light,
In the canvas of life, we paint it just right.

Dancing with dreams, in a playful parade,
We'll chase after magic, and never be swayed.
Through the broad horizons, come join in the fun,
For our journey together has only begun!

www.ingramcontent.com/pod-product-compliance
Lightning Source LLC
Chambersburg PA
CBHW062108280426
43661CB00086B/307